AN INTRODUCTION TO TRESCO

The Isles of Scilly lie some 28 miles west south west of Lands End. group of some 150 islets, only five of which are inhabited. Tresco is largest of these. It is approximately two miles long and one mile wide, and consists of some 735 acres with its highest point being only 135 feet. There are two fresh water pools on the island which are excellent bird watching areas.

The islands are lapped by the Gulf Stream and have equable temperatures, and adequate and regular rainfall which is coupled with an excellent sunshine record. In normal winters growth in sheltered places is hardly interrupted. Scilly has an average of over 350 days in the year with an air temperature above 50 F - a temperature at which plants will continue to grow. The influence of all this is reflected in the flora; the tropical garden on Tresco is a prime example.

There is no doubt that it is due to the foresight of the Dorrien-Smiths, who have leased the island from the Duchy of Cornwall for over 170 years, that Tresco has an indefinable something which the visitor should not miss. They have created and extended the tropical garden to blend in with the natural environment of white sandy beaches, and those who visit Tresco go away with such heady recollections that comparison with other such islands is impossible.

The helicopter landing at the heliport on Tresco

Most people visit Tresco by taking a boat trip from St Mary's, but Tresco itself can be a destination in its own right. It has its own regular helicopter service direct from Penzance, and the heliport can be found next to the Abbey Gardens. There is the Island Hotel in Old Grimsby, skillfully designed to blend in perfect harmony with the surrounding scenery of sea, rocks and sand. It boasts magnificent views with pleasant gardens, a heated swimming pool and a tennis court. There is also a centuries old Inn at New Grimsby, which has been thoroughly modernized and includes a swimming pool. There are also several holiday cottages available to let, and various properties available through timeshare. Details of all these can be obtained from the Estate Office.

Overlooking New Grimsby harbour

The island can be divided into two distinct halves, the northern half wild but full of interest, the southern half tropical, with a section in the centre joined by the two harbours of New Grimsby in the west, and Old Grimsby in the east which in the loosest way could be called the commercial area. This is where the inhabitants live in traditional stone cottages and where the church, school and the New Inn are located. The Post Office and the well stocked Tresco Stores are located on the site of the old seaplane base at New Grimsby.

The pleasure boats from St Mary's land their visitors at one of two places, depending on the state of the tide. The preferred place is at the harbour in New Grimsby, but this can only be reached through the channel between Bryher and Tresco; the other place is at Carn Near, the nearest point to St Mary's. New Grimsby is the ideal place to begin a walk around the Northern half, whilst Carn Near is much nearer the gardens and the beaches in the southern half.

The pleasure boats
picking up passengers
at Carn Near

The journey from St Mary's takes approximately twenty minutes and crosses an ancient inland valley where in prehistoric days the original inhabitants lived and tilled the ground to grow their corn. It would only take a fall of thirty feet in the level of the sea for Tresco, Bryher, St Martins and St Mary's to be once again joined together.

Tresco Abbey

As one approaches Tresco the first glimpses reveal a large granite building surrounded by trees. This is the Abbey, not a religious building but the home of the Dorrien-Smiths. It was built by Augustus Smith not long after he settled in the islands in 1834. At that time the surrounding hillside was as bare and windswept as any other island, but by planting trees that withstood the force of the winter winds he created a suntrap for the exotic plants he was gradually to introduce.

Low Tide at
New Grimsby

If the landing is to be at New Grimsby the boat passes between the islands of Bryher and Tresco. This is a shallow channel and on very low water it is still possible to walk from one island to the other. As one progresses up this channel on the right-hand side there is a rough granite monument. This is in memory of Augustus Smith although he is in fact buried in West Cornwall. It is near his beloved garden and commands a view of the islands he once ruled.

From the quay at New Grimsby the road follows along the shore for a short distance past the Gallery which houses regular art exhibitions, and a little further along is the New Inn. Here there is a road leading off to the left which will take you to Old Grimsby where the Island Hotel is located. To get to the gardens, keep to the coast road which leads to a group of estate buildings, built on a large area of concrete. This was originally laid for a seaplane base in the First World War. It was in 1917 that Curtis H12 'Large America' flying boats and Short 184 seaplanes were sent down from Plymouth. There were twenty two aircraft in all, and they were used for anti submarine patrols off the islands. Their presence meant that the German submarines had to stay deep to avoid being seen. Opposite these buildings you will see the Great Pool. Shortly after the estate buildings there is a division of roads, both of which will get you to the gardens.

THE ABBEY GARDENS

The left hand one enters an avenue of trees, whilst the right hand one follows the coast until you pass the heliport building shortly followed by the garden entrance. In the wooded walk are some fine trees, with several species of Eucalyptus and Southern Beeches from South America and Australia. There is also the Kauri Pine from New Zealand, one of the biggest trees in the world. At the end of the avenue the towers and turrets of Tresco Abbey come into view, the path veers left skirting the Abbey and then bears right, along the front of the Abbey. Follow this road along, with the Abbey on your right and the Abbey pool on your left and you will reach the entrance to the gardens.

The Agave sculpture by Tom Leaper at the bottom of the Mediterranean Garden

The bridge leading into the Gardens

The Summer House decorated with shell patterns by Lucy Dorrien-Smith

The new entrance with its complex of a shop, café, toilets and information centre leads over a bridge directly to the Mediterranean Garden. Here, at the base of the steps is a bronze sculpture of an agave with water running off its lower leaves. Further up the steps is a summer house beautifully decorated with shell patterns by Lucy Dorrien-Smith.

From here the top and middle terraces are easily reached. Laid out east to west the top terrace is noted for its display of Proteas from South Africa. There are several varieties, the King Protea , Protea Cynaroides being the most showy. The banks too are planted with a variety of heaths. From this terrace one gets a glimpse of the blue sea across to St Mary's and it culminates with a figurehead of Father Neptune. The head is that of a wooden figurehead from the SS Thames wrecked in Scilly in 1841. Its stone appearance is created by blowing fine sand onto wet paint.

Metrosideros excelsa *from New Zealand on the Top Terrace, in flower in the late summer*

A part of the Top Terrace Walk

The Protea's *from South Africa which come into flower in late summer*

Father Neptune, the figurehead from the SS Thames *wrecked in Scilly in 1841*

Before descending the steps from Neptune it is worth making a short diversion further along the path where there are many more plants to be seen, in an area known as Miss Innis' Garden which is a short loop into the hillside above.

*The Middle
Terrace and pool*

*The Summer House
seen from the pool
below the Middle
Terrace*

*The Middle Terrace
with its Summer House
seen from the Limpet
Midden*

By descending the steps the Middle Terrace is reached. This area has the true
Mediterranean feeling and in spring and summer is a maze of colour. The
summer house sited above a pond has figures on the pillars. An elephant's head
and a fist with trefoils are the insignia of the Dorrien-Smith family. The bank
above the terrace contains many agaves from Mexico. When these plants flower
their stem grows to a tremendous height.

*The Agaves in
the foreground
from Mexico*

The Middle Terrace

Blue Echiums from the Canaries and Cytisus Maderenses from Madeira, in full flower in the spring

Where the path along the Middle Terrace narrows is an old limpet midden supported by a granite wall, probably dating back to Roman times. This was substantiated when a gardener unearthed a Roman coin. The midden is composed of about six feet of limpet shells, limpets being the main diet of the inhabitants in the early centuries. It now makes a good viewpoint over the Middle Terrace. On the path on the opposite side are the blue flowers of the Echiums and on the top of the bank are Puya chelensis. When in flower the Blackbirds feed on its nectar and fly away with golden pollen dusted heads.

Puya Chilensis from Chile, at their best in May and June

View of the Middle Terrace past the limpet midden with a Fourcoya from Mexico in full display in the summer

*The marble
statue of 'Gaia'*

Returning along the Middle Terrace in an easterly direction, at the foot of Neptune Steps take a diversion and drop down a few more steps and turn to the right to see the marble statue of Gaia, sculptured by David Wynne. There are many plants in this area to view before returning to the foot of Neptunes Steps and turning right towards the large overhang of granite known as the Cliff.

*A blaze of colour
in the cliff*

Mesembryanthemum
*make a splash of colour
in the early summer*

It is richly planted
mostly with plants
from South Africa
with a scattering of
Canary Island
invaders. Dominant
are the aloes which
flower from
Christmas onwards,
Mesembryanthemum
in early summer as
well as Aeoniums
with their yellow
flower heads which
enjoy the baking sun.

Mesembryanthemum
and Senecio
glastiifolius *from
South Africa*

The Pebble Garden

Near the wooden frame at the base is an area known as Mexico where the Australian bottle brush flourish and now a range of South African cacti have been planted. From the frame one turns left into the pebble garden. The great wall on the western side has two flowers which stand out, the Red Lobster Claws from New Zealand and Bomarea caldasii from Ecuador. In the shady bottom corner of the Pebble Garden look for Saurauja subspinosa, a large leafed plant from Burma.

Bomarea caldasii *from Ecuador, flowers in mid-summer*

Clianthus puniceus *or Red Lobster Claws from New Zealand, flowers from mid-summer on*

The Saurauja subspinosa *from upper Burma, flowers in the autumn*

It is now not far from the Old Abbey which besides being colourful is one of the most historically important features on the island. The date of this ruin is uncertain but it is thought that Monks settled here sometime between 1042 and 1066. The priory dedicated to St Nicholas is first mentioned in a charter of 1120, by which Henry 1st granted all the churches of Scilly to the Benedictine Abbey at Tavistock in Devon. Under Tavistock's charge St Nicholas's Priory became the centre of the ecclesiastical administration which presided over the northern part of Scilly, the southern islands of St Mary's and St Agnes being under secular rule.

The Priory probably only housed two or three brethren, with servants living close by and farming adjoining land. St Helens Pool on the north east side of Tresco was probably the main harbour in Scilly at this time and the Priory may have collected tolls for the anchorage there. Hardly mentioned after the 15th century, the Priory was probably abandoned before the Reformation, when it did not even feature in a list of Tavistocks' possessions. Its abandonment was probably the result of increased attacks by pirates and raiders. Within the walls are some seventeenth and eighteenth century graves but the most interesting is a Roman gravestone, beneath the smaller of the two arches from the fifth or sixth century AD with roman capitals THI FILI COGVI. This is generally connected with the Celtic Christian missionaries from Ireland who sought to keep the faith alive in Britain at this time.

The remains of the Old Abbey

The steps down from
Father Neptune

The yellow flower of Aeonium *from the Canaries, with a surrounding of* Mesembryanthemum

Amaryllis Belladonna *from South Africa, found in many parts of the garden, it flowers in late summer*

Ipomoea learri *from tropical America, flowers from mid-summer on*

The bronze statue was sculptured by David Wynne. It portrays the three eldest children of Robert Dorrien-Smith, lessee of Tresco

From the Old Abbey take the road a short distance and turn into the long walk and then into Lighthouse walk where one sees the statues of three children. They depict the three elder children of Robert Dorrien-Smith, lessee of Tresco.

THE VALHALLA

Figureheads in the Valhalla

It is not far from here to the Valhalla. This is a very fine collection of figureheads from ships that have been wrecked in the islands. It exudes atmosphere as each figure is a ghost of the past. From their original position on the prow of a ship they have seen enough to tell many a story of shipwreck and disaster, of despair and death in violent waters. This collection was tracked down by Augustus Smith in ones and twos from barns, ditches and even from walls all over the islands in about 1840. They were originally housed on a veranda which faced east in the condition in which they had been found. The collection outgrew their location and many of the objects were not properly protected from the weather and were seriously decaying. In 1957 the restorations commenced with the building of the north facing wing, and the scientific treatment and replacement of rotten wood together with repainting in original colours so that today they probably represent the finest collection of figureheads in any one place.

The Salmon from a schooner wrecked in 1869

Forming a centerpiece is a large Mexican Eagle which is flanked on the left by a Spanish Lady and on the right a well dressed man brandishing a sword. In the collection of nearly sixty, a bust of a Highland Chieftain and the officer in Dress Uniform from the Volunteer, a local vessel are particularly worth seeing, as well as the Old Turk from the ship Bospherous. Also of particular interest are the two brass signal guns from the Schiller, a German passenger ship wrecked near the Bishop Rock Lighthouse with the loss of over 300 lives. A more recent addition has been a large brass cannon recovered in 1970 from the wreck of HMS Association. This was the flagship of Sir Cloudesley Shovell when he was returning from the siege of Toulon, in company with twenty other ships. He was unsure of his position in the entrance to the English Channel and before he realized it he was amongst the islands in thick fog and foul weather. In all, five ships foundered with the loss of over 2000 lives. Sir Cloudesley Shovell's body was washed ashore, and at first it was buried on the shore of St Mary's where it was found, but later it was re interred in Westminster Abbey.

Figurehead from the Bospherous, a brigantine known locally as the Old Turk

The central display in the Valhalla

THE SOUTHERN HALF

Agapanthus overlook the beaches

Once you have explored the gardens you can continue your journey around the southern half of the island. The garden is bounded by sandy dunes and silky white beaches, all of which add to the magical appearance of this fortunate isle. The dunes are thick with colourful heather in the summer, and studded with flowers- many reseeded from the garden – blue Agapanthus, pink Bella Donnas and Hottentot Fig growing wild amid the Marram Grass. In late September, clumps of Red Hot Poker , their red tops pointing to the sky, stand out like soldiers on guard over this paradise.

On the beaches above the tide lines are plants which can withstand being immersed in salt water from time to time. The Yellow Horned Poppy and the Thorn Apple are conspicuous, whilst the Sea Rocket, Prickly Saltwort and Orache blend into their surroundings. Higher up the beaches, Sea Holly and Spurges border the edge of the dunes, whilst Samphire, Mayweed and Sea Spurrey are rooted amongst any rocks that top the beach.

The white soft sands of Pentle Bay

The beaches below the tide line are jewels in themselves. Along the strand lines caused by the tides, shells of all colours and descriptions are found. They do not all originate from the beach on which they are found but are washed up into distinct lines. It is on these beaches that the much prized Cowrie shell locally known as the Guinea Money is found. It takes a keen eye and a lot of patience to find just a few.

All the area which bounds the garden could easily be classed a nature reserve, an area where the numerous birds and wild flowers add to nature's bounty. It is an area to be explored at one's leisure — an area which is beautiful and wild, and exerts a peace so difficult to find in today's society.

The shallow water at low tide makes it an ideal opportunity to explore

The crystal clear skies enhance the sense of peace

THE NORTHERN HALF

The northern half is bare and rugged; here the prevailing winds have fashioned the surroundings, leaving only stunted heather to gain a foothold in the more exposed west and north-west sides, whilst on the more sheltered north-east slopes falling down to the sea at Gimble Porth, wild rhododendrons have spread.

In winter these northern shores take an incessant pounding from the open Atlantic. The spray flies inland a considerable distance and the cliff face is washed bare by huge waves. In summer the heather bursts into flower in a great sheet of delicate colour and scents the air with its perfume.

The walk around the northern half begins at New Grimsby quay by taking the footpath alongside the shore to the left. The channel is a favourite place for yachtsmen and in the summer months many come to these shores, their boats of all shapes and sizes can be seen swinging to their anchors. After about half a mile one climbs a small hillock and Cromwell's Castle is viewed, with the depleted King Charles's Castle on the hill above. The view of Cromwell's Castle, in its unique situation of being almost surrounded by water becomes far more dramatic as one approaches closer; probably the best view is from King Charles's Castle above.

Yachts at anchor in New Grimsby Channel

King Charles's Castle was built 1550-54 to defend New Grimsby Channel. It had an earthwork defence on the landward side to protect if from attack across the headland. It actually fell to Admiral Blake's attack during the Civil War from this direction.

After this conquest Cromwell's Castle was built in 1651-52, because at this time the security of the islands was threatened by the hostile Dutch fleets. This was considered a better site to defend the channel than King Charles's Castle.

Cromwell's Castle

King Charles's Castle

Look across the heather towards Round Island

From King Charles's Castle the open downs look bare and uninteresting but in fact a lot of Scilly's early history is at one's feet. Glacial deposits, full of interest to geologists and antiquarians, are to be found on these downs. These stones were carried by ice floes from an east or north-east direction during the Pleistocene age and the floes touched the northern tips of St Martin's, Tresco, Bryher and St Agnes. It is, however, the strange way in which these foreign stones were swept across projecting headlands, rising more than 100 feet above sea level, that is so interesting. It seems that the sheet of ice gathered along the shores and, being pushed by wind and tide, broke to pieces on the headlands and these pieces were pushed inland. This appears to answer the question of why the stones are only found in certain narrow strips. Chalk flints, greensand cherts, soft red sandstone, fragments of hardened killas and well-rounded pebbles of harder sandstone are all to be found. Flints are the most abundant of all the stones.

It was on these downs that the prospectors made cuttings in their efforts to find tin. Borlase in his survey of 1796, noted a vein of tin two feet wide in the cliff face at Gun Well, this is a large cavern situated on the north-west point.

However, long before this period these downs were used by the Bronze Age people to bury their dead in stone-built barrows. Only one now exists and this is on Tregarthen Hill. It is in good condition and well worth finding. It is thought a lot of barrows were pillaged for their stone when the building of the castles was in progress.

Before finding this barrow on Tregarthen Hill it is probably easier to walk to Piper's Hole. One walks in a straight line from King Charles's Castle towards Round Island lighthouse, and just to the right of a granite carn there is a narrow channel in the rocky coast about sixty yards long. This leads from the water's edge to a small black cavity in the cliff face, which is the entrance to Piper's Hole. Gaining access to the entrance is difficult, and the boulders on entering are very slippery, so it is no place for the unsure of foot. Some form of lighting is necessary; candles give the best atmospheric effect. After scrambling over large boulders the cave begins to descend and after about thirty-five yards a freshwater lake is encountered. The height of the chamber rises considerably at this point and if one places the candles on each side, the reflections in the water, helped buy a penetration of daylight illuminating the top, it becomes an enchanting sight. This feeling can be reversed if there is a heavy ground swell running as one can hear the rumble of boulders moving about on the seabed, making one feel an awesome respect for the sea, and sends shivers down the spine. Indeed in winter the sea actually enters this cavern. If one is able to cross the lake by an inflatable of some kind, the cave continues on for a further fifty to sixty yards and the floor is composed of small particles of granite, making the going very much easier. This cave is supposed by some to have been a tin mine of Phoenician days, but no veins have been found in recent times and the fissure is more likely to have been caused by the Atlantic waves eroding a fault in the granite.

Piper's Hole

On regaining the surface the path continues eastward. One climbs the slope of Tregarthen Hill and before dropping down to the seclusion of Gimble Porth turn inland and gain the top of the hill. This is where the ancient burial chamber is sited. This grave dates back to the early Bronze Age 1900-1500BC and is built in the tradition of the early megalithic culture. This culture spread up from the Mediterranean along the Iberian coast, to Brittany and then to Scilly, Ireland and Scotland, and there are also parallels in Egypt. There is, therefore, evidence for trade and contact between Scilly and the Mediterranean in Bronze Age times. In the first scientific excavation of one of these tombs it was found burials at first were by interments and later by cremation. In one grave the remains of at least seventy vessels, each one with cremated remains of one person were unearthed.

The burial chamber on Tregarthen Hill

From the top of this hill it is worth taking in the view in front of you, as in early times this was probably the centre of trade for Scilly. From the left, standing aloof is Men-a-Vaur, gaunt and stark, almost inaccessible and now the home of countless seabirds during the nesting season — puffins, razorbills, guillemots, kittiwakes, fulmars, shags and cormorants. Next comes Round Island with its lighthouse. Before its erection there were three immense burial mounds on the top. Slightly nearer is St Helen's, home of St Elidius. Monks carried on extensive trading from here as St Helen's Pool was the chief harbour in Scilly in medieval times. On this island there are the remains of a church, with nave, chancel and north aisle; there is also an oratory with an altar at its east end. There are several primitive huts, one circular and the others rectangular, as well as massive enclosure walls. The church is of medieval date but the huts have the appearance of greater age. The site is typical of the remote spots on the islands off the west coast of Ireland, which were selected by early Christian hermits. This is not to be confused with the stone building, still standing to roof level with a chimney, in the centre of the island, which is the old pest house. Regulations for the quarantine issued in August 1805 stated that all vessels coming to Britain via Scilly were to make for St Helen's Pool where those aboard were carefully inspected to detect any diseases.

Rhododendrons overlook Gimble Porth

The island in the foreground is Northwethel with its castle-like carns. Its main claim to historic fame is that this is where Admiral Blake first landed in Scilly (by mistake). During the Civil War the islands had remained in Royalist hands, however in 1651, hastened by the presence of a Dutch Fleet, Parliament decided to reduce them. It was Admiral Blake who was sent, and, with due regard to the Royalist defences he decided the best place to attack was at Old Grimsby where the only defence was the Old Blockhouse. After his initial mistake of landing on Northwethel he landed at Old Grimsby, took the Blockhouse and then overran King Charles's Castle. His next move was to construct a battery above Carn Near, known as Oliver's Fort from which he could fire on any shipping using the Sound between Tresco and St Mary's. So without having to attack St Mary's he forced the Royalists to surrender.

The background to this panorama we have before us is the island of Teän with St Martin's and the Eastern Isles further in the distance. In former years the whole centre of this lagoon would at times have been filled with sailing ships at anchor.

From Tregarthen Hill the path drops down to the seclusion of Gimble Porth. This porth has a backdrop of wild Rhododendrons and in the spring these burst into flower giving the entire side of the hill a beautiful pink hue.

The Island Hotel

The path skirts the Island Hotel and passes along the shore to Old Grimsby where a few houses, the school, the community centre and the church are located. The school, on the edge of an open green, educates Tresco and Bryher children until the age of eleven, when they are transferred to the secondary base on St Mary's as weekly borders. The Church of St Nicholas, the patron saint of seafarers, was built in 1882 to the memory of Augustus Smith. It was designed by his successor T A Dorrien-Smith and built by island masons and carpenters.

The Church of St Nicholas

Flanking the bay at Old Grimsby are the remains of an old Blockhouse. Its date of building is uncertain but in 1554 there is a record of a fortification here. It consists of a rectangular platform paved with stone, raised high on a carn overlooking St Helen's Pool and the harbour of Old Grimsby. This is the defence that Blake had to overcome when he landed on Tresco in 1651. A road across the island joins the bays of Old Grimsby and New Grimsby where the exploration of the northern half began. The road back to New Grimsby passes some of the cultivated ground belonging to the estate in which they grow their early spring flowers. The farm consists of some 150 acres some 100 of which are grassland. The fields are protected by fast-growing fences of Veronica, Escallonia and Pittosporum, and the main crop of flowers is the narcissus, Soleil d'Or which favours the light sandy soils of Scilly. The flower season runs from early October through to the middle of March and 60% of the flowers are sold through the island farmer's consortium Mainland Marketing, who deal directly with supermarkets and large retail florists. The remaining 40% are sent to wholesale markets such as Covent Garden. The island also has its own herd of approximately 20 cattle and has a resident Limousin bull. Tresco beef can be found on the islands menus and has a fine reputation for it's quality.

The Blockhouse is prominent on the hill above the beach

The cattle grazing on the coastline

*The view from the
Blockhouse looking
towards St Helens
and Teän*

Having visited Tresco I trust that you have been able to enjoy some of it's
enchantment, have appreciated its contrasts from the rugged north to the
tropical south, and above all have enjoyed its peace and quiet away from crowds
and traffic, where the wild birds in Tresco garden will eat from your hand, and
where tomorrow beckons another such day.